3 Write as semibreves (whole notes) the scales named below. [10]

A major, descending, with key signature.

D minor, ascending, without key signature but adding any necessary sharp or flat signs.

Which form of the minor scale have you used? ....

4 (a) Rewrite these bass clef notes in the treble clef, keeping the pitch the same. The first answer is given. [10]

(b) In which major key are all these notes found? ....

5 Rewrite the following in notes of *half* the value, beginning as shown. Remember to group (beam) the notes correctly where necessary. [10]

Dvořák

6 Add the correct clef and key signature to each of these tonic triads.

10

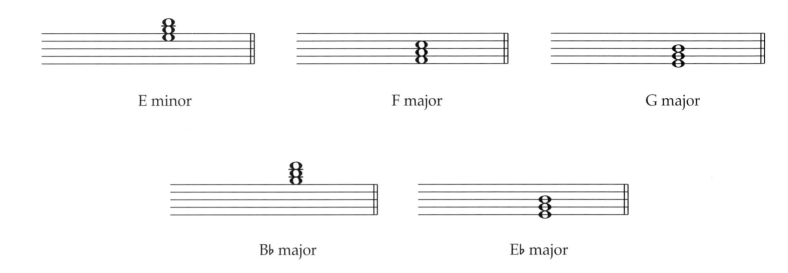

E minor   F major   G major

Bb major   Eb major

7 Rewrite the following melody, grouping (beaming) the notes correctly.

10

Haydn

4

8 Look at this melody by Grieg and then answer the questions below.

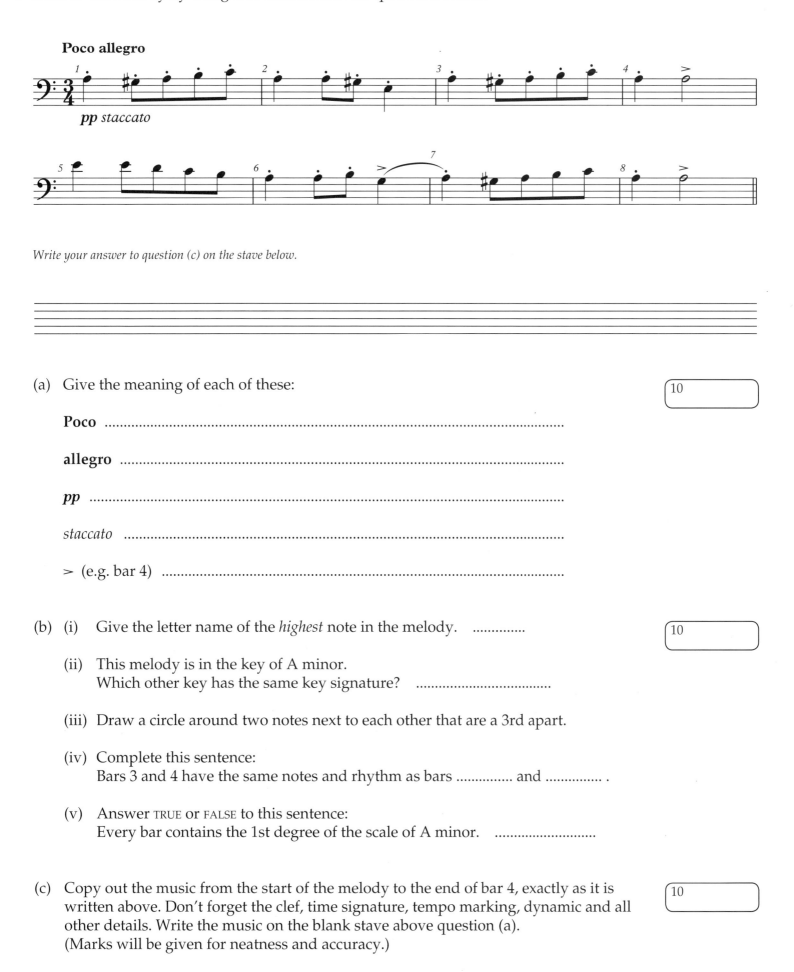

Write your answer to question (c) on the stave below.

(a) Give the meaning of each of these:

Poco ....

allegro ....

pp ....

staccato ....

> (e.g. bar 4) ....

| 10 |

(b) (i) Give the letter name of the *highest* note in the melody. ....

(ii) This melody is in the key of A minor.
Which other key has the same key signature? ....

(iii) Draw a circle around two notes next to each other that are a 3rd apart.

(iv) Complete this sentence:
Bars 3 and 4 have the same notes and rhythm as bars .... and ....

(v) Answer TRUE or FALSE to this sentence:
Every bar contains the 1st degree of the scale of A minor. ....

| 10 |

(c) Copy out the music from the start of the melody to the end of bar 4, exactly as it is written above. Don't forget the clef, time signature, tempo marking, dynamic and all other details. Write the music on the blank stave above question (a).
(Marks will be given for neatness and accuracy.)

| 10 |

Theory Paper   Grade 2   2013   B

Duration 1¹/₂ hours

TOTAL MARKS
100

Candidates should answer ALL questions.
Write your answers on this paper – no others will be accepted.
Answers must be written clearly and neatly – otherwise marks may be lost.

1 Add the missing bar-lines to these two melodies. The first bar-line is given in each.

10

Cornet

Smetana

2 Write a four-bar rhythm using the given opening.

10

3 Rewrite this melody in the treble clef, keeping the pitch the same. The first bar is given.

10

Musorgsky

4 Add the correct clef and any necessary sharp or flat signs to make each of the scales named below. Do *not* use key signatures.

`10`

A minor

Which form of the minor scale have you used? ....

B♭ major

5 (a) Give the letter name of each of the notes marked *, including the sharp sign where necessary. The first answer is given.

`10`

E
....

(b) Give the time name (e.g. crotchet or quarter note) of the *longest* note in the melody. ....

6 *After* each note write a *higher* note to form the named *melodic* interval, as shown in the first answer. The key is E♭ major.

`10`

5th   8th/8ve   3rd

4th   2nd   7th

7 Write the time values
in the correct order, from the *shortest* to the *longest*. The first answer is given.

`10`

....

8 Look at this melody, adapted from a piece by Donaudy, and then answer the questions below.

Write your answer to question (c) on the stave below.

(a) Give the meaning of each of these:

    Allegro ....

    pp ....

    allargando (bar 3) ....

    ⎺⎺ (e. g. bar 3) ....

    dim. (bar 4) ....

10

(b) (i) How many bars contain semiquavers (16th notes)? ....

    (ii) Answer TRUE or FALSE to this sentence:
        The first note of bar 4 should be played with a slight pressure. ....

    (iii) This melody is in the key of D major. Name the degree
        of the scale (e.g. 1st, 2nd) of the first note in the melody. ....

    (iv) Draw a circle around a note in this melody that is *not* in the key of D major.

    (v) In which bar is the performer told to play 'in time'? Bar ....

10

(c) Copy out the music from the start of bar 3 to the end of the extract, exactly as it is
written above. Don't forget the clef, key signature, dynamics and all other details.
Write the music on the blank stave above question (a).
(Marks will be given for neatness and accuracy.)

10

Theory Paper   Grade 2   2013   C

Duration 1¹/₂ hours

Candidates should answer ALL questions.
Write your answers on this paper – no others will be accepted.
Answers must be written clearly and neatly – otherwise marks may be lost.

TOTAL MARKS
100

1 Add the time signature to each of these five melodies.

10

Sullivan

Liszt

Chopin

Hellendaal

Telemann

2 Write a four-bar rhythm using the given opening.

10

3 Name each key as shown by its key signature. The first answer is given.   [10]

..Bb.. major   .... major   .... minor

.... major   .... major   .... minor

4 Give the number (e.g. 2nd, 3rd) of each of these harmonic intervals, as shown in the first answer. The key is G major.   [10]

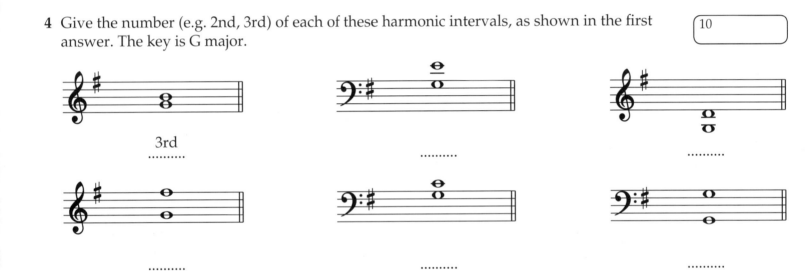

3rd   ....

....

5 (a) Name the degree of the scale (e.g. 2nd, 3rd) of each of the notes marked *, as shown in the first answer. The key is Bb major.   [10]

Haydn

2nd   ....

(b) How many quavers (eighth notes) are the rests in the last bar worth in total?  ....

6 Rewrite this melody *without* using a key signature. Remember to include flat or natural signs where they are needed. The key is B♭ major and the first bar is given.

Sullivan (adapted)

7 Add the correct clef and any necessary sharp or flat signs to make each of the scales named below. Do *not* use key signatures. 10

E minor

Which form of the minor scale have you used? ....

F major

8 Look at this melody by Lehmann and then answer the questions below.

Write your answer to question (c) on the stave below.

(a) Give the meaning of each of these:

Andante ....

molto ....

legato ....

p (e.g. bar 1) ....

cresc. (e.g. bar 4) ....

(b) (i) This melody is in the key of D minor. Draw a bracket (⌐———⌐) over three notes next to each other that form the tonic triad in this key.

(ii) Draw a circle around a note in this melody that is *not* in the key of D minor.

(iii) Give the letter name of the first note in bar 4. ....

(iv) Complete this sentence:
Bar 1 has the same notes and rhythm as bar ....

(v) How many times does the rhythm ♪♪♪♪ occur? ....

(c) Copy out the music from the start of bar 5 to the end of the melody, exactly as it is written above. Don't forget the clef, key signature, dynamics and all other details. Write the music on the blank stave above question (a).
(Marks will be given for neatness and accuracy.)

10

10

10

Theory Paper   Grade 2   2013   S

Duration 1¹/₂ hours

Candidates should answer ALL questions.
Write your answers on this paper – no others will be accepted.
Answers must be written clearly and neatly – otherwise marks may be lost.

TOTAL MARKS
100

1   Add the missing bar-lines to these two melodies. The first bar-line is given in each.

10

Haydn

Schütz

2   Write a four-bar rhythm using the given opening.

10

3 (a) Name the degree of the scale (e.g. 2nd, 3rd) of each of the notes marked *, as shown in the first answer. The key is A major.

Linley

5th ....

(b) Give the time name (e.g. crotchet or quarter note) of the *shortest* rest in the melody ....

4 Add the correct rest(s) at the places marked * in these two melodies to make each bar complete.

Wagner

Schreker

5 Rewrite this melody in the bass clef, keeping the pitch the same. The first three notes are given.

Mozart